DATE DUE

CASEY
at the
BAT

By
Ernest Lawrence Thayer

Illustrated by Paul Frame

Prentice-Hall, Inc., Englewood Cliffs, N. J.

E
811
7H A

10   9   8

Casey at the Bat, by Ernest Lawrence Thayer
illustrated by Paul Frame

© 1964 by Prentice Hall, Inc., Englewood Cliffs, N.J.

Library of Congress Catalog Card Number: 64-13248
Printed in the United States of America
ISBN 0-13-120402-5 (pbk.); ISBN 0-13-120410-6

Prentice-Hall International, Inc., *London* / Prentice-Hall
of Australia, Pty., Ltd., *Sydney* / Prentice-Hall of
Canada, Ltd., *Toronto* / Prentice-Hall France, S.A.R.L.,
Paris / Prentice-Hall of India (Private) Ltd., *New Delhi* /
Prentice-Hall of Japan, Inc., Tokyo

It looked extremely rocky
    for the Mudville nine that day;
The score stood two to four,
    with but one inning left to play.

So, when Cooney died at second,
and Burrows did the same,
A pallor wreathed the features
of the patrons of the game.

A straggling few got up to go,
leaving there the rest,
With that hope which springs eternal
within the human breast.

For they thought: "If only Casey
could get a whack at that,"
They'd put even money now,
with Casey at the bat.

But Flynn preceded Casey,
    and likewise so did Blake,
And the former was a pudd'n,
    and the latter was a fake.

So on that stricken multitude
a deathlike silence sat;
For there seemed but little chance
of Casey's getting to the bat.

But Flynn let drive a single,
to the wonderment of all.
And the much-despised Blakey
"tore the cover off the ball."

And when the dust had lifted,
    and they saw what had occurred,
There was Blakey safe at second,
    and Flynn a-huggin' third.

Then from the gladdened multitude
went up a joyous yell—
It rumbled in the mountaintops,
it rattled in the dell;

It struck upon the hillside
    and rebounded on the flat;
For Casey, mighty Casey,
    was advancing to the bat.

There was ease in Casey's manner
as he stepped into his place,
There was pride in Casey's bearing
and a smile on Casey's face;

And when responding to the cheers
he lightly doffed his hat,
No stranger in the crowd could doubt
'twas Casey at the bat.

Ten thousand eyes were on him
    as he rubbed his hands with dirt,
Five thousand tongues applauded
    when he wiped them on his shirt;

Then when the writhing pitcher
ground the ball into his hip,
Defiance gleamed from Casey's eye,
a sneer curled Casey's lip.

And now the leather-covered sphere
came hurtling through the air,
And Casey stood a-watching it
in haughty grandeur there.

Close by the sturdy batsman
the ball unheeded sped;
"That ain't my style," said Casey.
"Strike one," the umpire said.

From the benches, black with people,
   there went up a muffled roar,
Like the beating of the storm waves
   on the stern and distant shore.

"Kill him! Kill the umpire!"
 shouted someone on the stand;
And it's likely they'd have killed him
 had not Casey raised his hand.

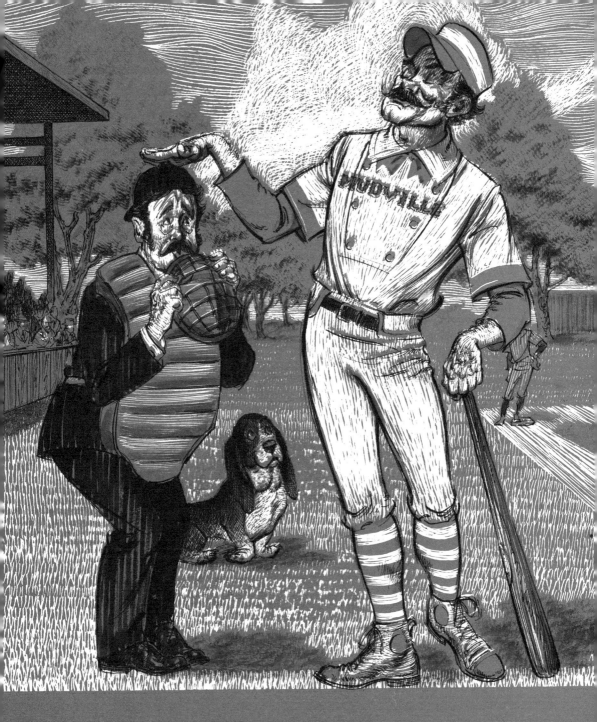

With a smile of Christian charity
    great Casey's visage shone;
He stilled the rising tumult,
    he made the game go on;

He signaled to the pitcher,
  and once more the spheroid flew;
But Casey still ignored it,
  and the umpire said, "Strike two."

"Fraud!" cried the maddened thousands,
and the echo answered "Fraud!"
But one scornful look from Casey
and the audience was awed;

They saw his face grow stern and cold,
they saw his muscles strain,
And they knew that Casey wouldn't let
the ball go by again.

The sneer is gone from Casey's lips,
   his teeth are clenched in hate,
He pounds with cruel vengeance
   his bat upon the plate;

And now the pitcher holds the ball,
and now he lets it go,
And now the air is shattered
by the force of Casey's blow.

Oh, somewhere in this favored land
   the sun is shining bright,
The band is playing somewhere,
   and somewhere hearts are light;

And somewhere men are laughing,
   and somewhere children shout,
But there is no joy in Mudville—
   mighty Casey has struck out.

Scores of baseball players have claimed to be the author's model for "Casey." One of them, Daniel M. Casey, of Silver Spring, Maryland (who struck out for the Phillies in a game against the Giants in 1887) insisted that *he* was Casey until the day of his death in 1938.

But William Lawrence Thayer, the author, always said he had no particular player in mind when he wrote CASEY AT THE BAT.

This narrative poem is almost as old as baseball itself. It was first published in *The San Francisco Examiner* on June 3, 1888, and DeWolf Hopper, a vaudeville actor, made it famous by reciting it on stages across the land.